Food Dudes

CLARENCE BIRDSEYE:

Frozen Food Innovator

Joanne Mattern

**Checkerboard
Library**

An Imprint of Abdo Publishing
www.abdopublishing.com

www.abdopublishing.com

Published by Abdo Publishing, a division of ABDO, PO Box 398166, Minneapolis, Minnesota 55439. Copyright © 2015 by Abdo Consulting Group, Inc. International copyrights reserved in all countries. No part of this book may be reproduced in any form without written permission from the publisher. Checkerboard Library™ is a trademark and logo of Abdo Publishing.

Printed in the United States of America, North Mankato, Minnesota.
052014
092014

Cover Photos: Getty Images
Interior Photos: Alamy pp. 10, 13; courtesy Birds Eye Foods LLC pp. 11, 26; Corbis pp. 15, 21, 25;
    Getty Images p. 1; Granger Collection pp. 5, 17; Public Domain p. 7; Library of Congress p. 9;
    Neil Klinepier p. 23; United States Patent and Trademark Office pp. 18–19

Series Coordinator: BreAnn Rumsch
Editors: Megan M. Gunderson, BreAnn Rumsch
Art Direction & Cover Design: Neil Klinepier

Library of Congress Control Number: 2014941017

Mattern, Joanne, 1963-
  Clarence Birdseye : frozen food innovator / Joanne Mattern.
     p. cm. -- (Food dudes)
  ISBN 978-1-62403-492-3
  1. Birdseye, Clarence, 1886-1956--Juvenile literature. 2. Frozen foods industry--United States-
-History--Juvenile literature. 3. Inventors--United States--Biography--Juvenile literature. 4.
Businessmen--United States--Biography--Juvenile literature. I. Title.
  HD9217.U52B576 2015
  338.7'66402853092--dc23
                                2014941017

Contents

Brooklyn Boy

Chances are, your home's freezer is full of yummy items that can be prepared in minutes. Clarence Birdseye made this possible. He found new ways to freeze foods and bring them to the public. His inventions changed the food industry. Today, we depend on convenient foods to make our busy lives easier.

Clarence Frank Birdseye was born in Brooklyn, New York, on December 9, 1886. Clarence was named for his father, who was a lawyer. His mother was Ada Underwood Birdseye. She was the daughter of an inventor and manufacturer. Clarence grew up in a big family. He was one of eight children.

In addition to their home in Brooklyn, the Birdseye family had a farm. It was on Long Island in New York. Clarence and his brothers and sisters enjoyed many summers there.

Clarence Birdseye

Growing Up

As a boy, Clarence spent most of his time outside. At the farm, he explored the fields and the woods. He also went down to the beach and roamed along the seashore.

Clarence loved nature. He learned about animals and how they live in the wild. Clarence also studied taxidermy. He became skilled at stuffing and mounting animals for display.

After several years in Brooklyn, the Birdseye family moved to Montclair, New Jersey. There, Clarence discovered he was interested in more than just animals. He also liked cooking! So, Clarence signed up for a cooking class at school.

Clarence graduated from Montclair High School in 1908. Next, he decided to attend Amherst College in Amherst, Massachusetts. Most of the men in his family had attended this school.

Today's Montclair High School is much larger than the one Clarence attended.

Odd Jobs

Clarence had to help his family pay for his education. So before starting college, he worked in an office in New York City, New York. Soon, Clarence found more unusual ways to make money in the city. He trapped frogs and rats! He sold the frogs to the Bronx Zoo for reptile food. He sold the rats to a scientist at Columbia University.

At Amherst, Clarence studied many types of sciences related to animals. He enjoyed learning about mammals, birds, and insects. His friends even nicknamed him Bugs. Then in 1910, Clarence had to drop out of college. He and his family could no longer afford to pay for his education.

After leaving school, Clarence needed to find work. He wanted a job that put his knowledge of animals to good use. He began working as a field naturalist for the U.S. Department of Agriculture.

This job required Clarence to travel through Arizona and New Mexico. There, he collected birds and other animals for the government to study.

Life was difficult out in the desert. But Clarence didn't mind. His surroundings were interesting. And, he used his cooking skills to survive. One time, he made a tasty meat soup. It contained mice, chipmunks, rats, and gophers!

While in the desert, Clarence kept detailed journals of his discoveries.

Fur Trader

Even today, much of Labrador remains unpopulated wilderness.

In 1912, Birdseye met Eleanor Gannett while in Washington, D.C. They soon fell in love. Birdseye wanted to marry her. But, he knew he couldn't afford to support a family.

Then, Birdseye learned that fur traders in Canada made a good living. So, he joined the Hudson Bay Trading Company. The next year, he moved to Labrador in eastern Canada. There were many wild animals in Labrador. Birdseye bought and sold their furs for money.

At that time, Labrador offered Birdseye much adventure. There were no cars or trains in the wilderness. So during the summer

Birdseye wore sealskin to stay warm during Labrador's cold winters.

months, Birdseye traveled by boat. In the winter months, he traveled by dogsled.

Eventually, Birdseye had enough money to marry. Back in the United States, he and Eleanor wed on August 21, 1915. The next year, the Birdseyes welcomed their first son, Kellogg. Birdseye wanted to return to Labrador. So just a few weeks later, he moved his family there.

Life in the Wild

Birdseye was happy to have his wife and son with him in Labrador. However, he worried about how to take care of them. There were no stores in the area. The family had to catch or grow all their own food. Birdseye needed to find a way to store food and keep it fresh.

Birdseye observed how the native Inuit people provided for themselves. They ice fished in winter. At that time of year, the air was extremely cold. It froze the fish as soon as they were pulled out of the water!

Later, Birdseye thawed and ate some of this fish. He noticed it tasted almost as good as fresh fish. Birdseye experimented with bird and caribou meat as well. He tasted meat frozen at different times of year. Birdseye discovered that meat frozen in the extreme winter cold tasted best.

Birdseye used inspiration from the Inuit fishing method to later create his freezing inventions.

Understanding Freezing

Birdseye thought about his experiments with frozen foods. He realized that meat froze most quickly in extreme winter cold. His science background helped him understand why this mattered.

When food freezes slowly, large ice crystals form. These large crystals damage the food, making it look and taste bad. When food freezes quickly, only small ice crystals can form. These do not damage the food the way large crystals do.

At the time, frozen food was not popular. It simply didn't taste good. Birdseye concluded this was because the food was frozen too slowly. He believed people would eat more frozen food if it tasted better. So, he kept experimenting.

Next, Birdseye tried freezing vegetables. He washed some cabbages in salt water and froze them in the cold air. Later, he thawed out some cabbage and ate it. The cabbage tasted great!

Now Birdseye was certain that food must be frozen quickly. Then, meats and vegetables would look and taste fresh when cooked. Birdseye thought about starting a frozen-foods business. However, his plan had to wait.

Birdseye had a curious mind.
He was also persistent when
conducting experiments.

Trial and Error

In 1917, the United States entered **World War I**. That same year, Birdseye and his family moved back to the United States. For a time, the family settled in Washington, D.C. There, Birdseye held jobs with several government organizations. These included the U.S. Housing Office and the U.S. Fisheries Association.

Meanwhile, Birdseye did not forget about his business idea. In 1922, he started his own company in New York City. It was called Birdseye Seafood Inc. But Birdseye could not convince shoppers to try his frozen fish. The company soon failed.

Still, Birdseye was not discouraged. He continued working on his experiments at home. In 1923, he invested in an electric fan, a few buckets of **brine**, and some cakes of ice. The materials cost him seven dollars.

With these items, Birdseye soon discovered a way to flash freeze foods. First, fresh food was packaged in small cardboard cartons. Then, they were frozen between two metal surfaces chilled to -40 degrees Fahrenheit (-40°C). Birdseye received a **patent** for this method in 1924.

Eventually, Birdseye's flash freezing method made it possible to freeze all kinds of foods.

BIRDS EYE HARVEST OF TIME-SAVERS FOR THIS WEEKEND

Save time **this weekend** with these delicious **time-saving** Birds Eye foods!

MONEY SAVERS TOO

Here's an invitation to save money on Birds Eye time-savers. Send coupon to Birds Eye Money Savers, P.O. Box 1222,* Kankakee, Ill., for 4 coupons (1 set to a family) each worth 5¢ off on the purchase of one package of any Birds Eye product.

Name_____

Address_____

Grocer's Name_____

Grocer's Address_____

*In Canada: P.O. Box 2170, Toronto. Offer good in U.S., Canada, Hawaii, Puerto Rico, and Alaska.
Favorites from General Foods . . . pioneer of frozen foods

Some freeze food...
BIRDS EYE FREEZES FLAVOR

That's why more people buy Birds Eye than any other frozen food.

Watch your grocer's ads for Birds Eye's better buys—today!

The Quick Freeze Machine

In 1924, Birdseye met several businessmen who believed in his freezing method. They agreed to work with him. Together, they formed the General Seafoods Company. It was located in Gloucester, Massachusetts. The company packaged and sold boxes of frozen fish.

At General Seafoods, Birdseye was able to improve his machinery. By 1926, he had invented the double belt freezer. Birdseye called it his Quick Freeze Machine. It could freeze large quantities of food. Fish was still packaged in cartons and pressed between metal plates. But, the new plates were hollow and chilled to -25 degrees Fahrenheit (-32°C).

This method froze food very quickly! It could freeze meat in only 90 minutes. Fruits and vegetables took just 30 minutes. Soon, the new machine was freezing all kinds of different foods. Birdseye was granted a **patent** for his Quick Freeze Machine in 1930.

Birdseye's Quick Freeze Machine was huge. It weighed 20 tons (18 t)!

Building a Brand

In 1929, Birdseye and his partners sold General Seafoods. A large food business called Postum bought it for $22 million. Postum changed the General Seafoods name to Birds Eye Frosted Food Company. Postum also changed its own name to General Foods Corporation. Birdseye became wealthy from the sale. However, he remained with General Foods to work on research and development.

General Foods knew it had to convince shoppers that Birds Eye foods were appealing. So in 1930, the company launched a large advertising campaign. On March 6, General Foods began selling the Birds Eye brand. The choices included vegetables, fruit, fish, oysters, and meat.

At first, Birds Eye foods were only available in 18 stores in Springfield, Massachusetts. Most stores couldn't afford the necessary equipment to sell frozen foods. So in 1934, Birdseye hired a company to build special display freezers. He rented these freezer cases to store owners so they would sell his food. By 1937, about 2,000 stores were selling Birds Eye products.

Still, it was impossible to ship frozen food far away. The packages would thaw during the trip. Birdseye had an answer to this problem as well. In 1944, he began renting refrigerated railroad cars. With those, Birds Eye frozen products sold all over the country.

In grocery stores, freezer cases allow you to easily see the cold items you want.

Convenient Food

Before **World War II**, canning had been one of the most common ways to preserve food. But during the war, tin for cans was hard to come by. Freezing became a better option than canning. People soon began buying more frozen food products.

By the late 1940s, home freezers were popular. Frozen foods became common in home kitchens. They made it more convenient for busy families to eat healthy food. By 1959, the Birds Eye brand offered more than 100 items to choose from.

Meanwhile, Birdseye experimented with other methods of preserving food. He knew that quickly freezing food helped preserve its flavor. He decided that quickly **dehydrating** food might work the same way.

By 1949, Birdseye had developed a process called anhydrous dehydration. It removed water from foods, which made the foods shrink. Then, the foods could be packaged in small boxes. This method made food convenient to store and carry.

Today, frozen Birds Eye
products provide families
with many healthy,
easy-to-prepare meals.

Inventor at Heart

Birdseye had many other interests besides food preservation. While working on his freezer inventions, he also started the Birdseye Electric Company. He created special lightbulbs used for display lighting in stores. He also invented heat lamps to keep food warm in restaurants.

For fun, Birdseye invented an electric fishing reel. It helped commercial fishermen catch more fish. He also invented a harpoon gun for whale hunting.

In 1953, Birdseye started working on a new idea. He traveled to Peru to study paper manufacturing. After two years, Birdseye found a way to improve the process. He used sugar cane waste to make paper pulp. This decreased the papermaking process from 9 hours to 12 minutes!

Birdseye continued working for the rest of his life. He never stopped coming up with new inventions. Eventually, he held more than 300 U.S. and foreign **patents**.

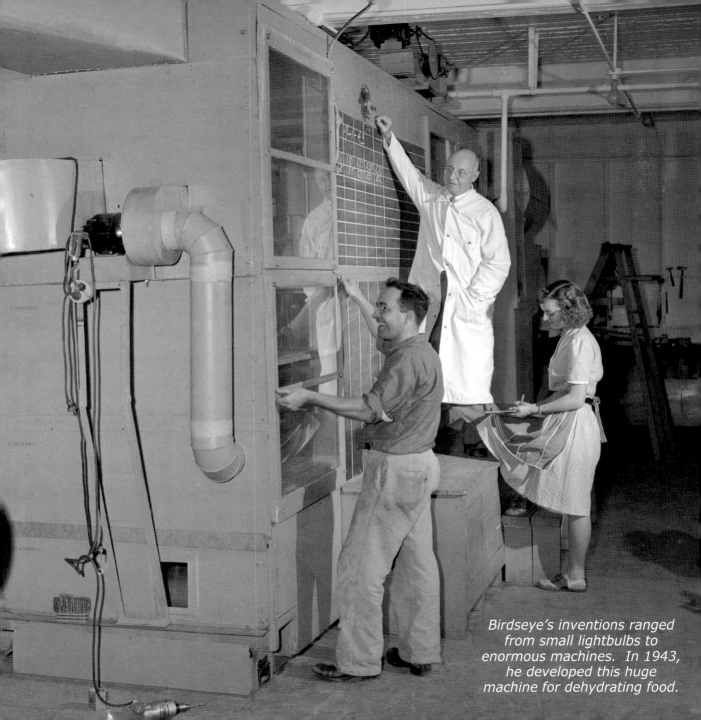

Birdseye's inventions ranged from small lightbulbs to enormous machines. In 1943, he developed this huge machine for dehydrating food.

Many Interests

Birdseye did more than just invent things. He once said, "I have more hobbies than the law allows." He was interested in gardening, cooking, and entertaining. He also liked to play Chinese checkers.

Birdseye was a writer, too. He wrote many articles. Birdseye even wrote a story about Labrador called "Hard Luck on the Labrador."

Together, he and Eleanor wrote a book called *Growing Woodland Plants*. It was published in 1951.

The Birdseyes were married for more than 40 years. They had four children together. In addition to Kellogg, the Birdseyes had another son named Henry. They also had two daughters named Ruth and Eleanor.

On October 7, 1956, Clarence Birdseye was in New York City at the Gramercy Park Hotel. He died there of a heart attack. Almost 50 years later, Birdseye was recognized for his work. In 2005, he was **inducted** into the National Inventors Hall of Fame.

Clarence Birdseye did not invent frozen food. However, he created a better way to freeze and sell it to consumers. His work made it easier for people to have healthy food anytime. In this way, Birdseye forever changed the way people eat.

Birdseye made one of the most important developments in the food industry.

Timeline

1886	On December 9, Clarence Frank Birdseye was born in Brooklyn, New York.
1908	Clarence graduated from Montclair High School in Montclair, New Jersey.
1915	Birdseye married Eleanor Gannett on August 21.
1916	Birdseye moved his wife and son to Labrador, Canada.
1924	Birdseye patented his method of flash freezing foods; he helped form the General Seafoods Company in Gloucester, Massachusetts.
1926	Birdseye invented the Quick Freeze Machine.
1929	Birdseye sold General Seafoods to Postum; General Seafoods became the Birds Eye Frosted Food Company and Postum became General Foods Corporation.
1930	Birdseye patented his Quick Freeze Machine; General Foods began selling the Birds Eye brand.
1949	Birdseye discovered anhydrous dehydration.
1953	Birdseye traveled to Peru, where he studied paper manufacturing.
1956	On October 7, Clarence Birdseye died in New York City, New York.

Family Legend

A family story explains where Clarence Birdseye's unusual last name came from.

Long ago, one of Birdseye's ancestors worked for a queen of England. One day, a hawk swooped down toward the queen. The man saved her by shooting an arrow through the bird's eye. The queen gave the man the name "Bird's Eye." From then on, he was known by that name.

When Birdseye's frozen foods became a brand, the inventor's name was an obvious choice for the brand name. The Birdseye family legend lent itself to the brand's logo. Every Birds Eye package is marked by a swooping bird.

Glossary

brine - very salty water.

dehydrate - to remove water from something, such as food.

induct - to admit as a member.

patent - the exclusive right granted to a person to make or sell an invention. This right lasts for a certain period of time.

World War I - from 1914 to 1918, fought in Europe. Great Britain, France, Russia, the United States, and their allies were on one side. Germany, Austria-Hungary, and their allies were on the other side.

World War II - from 1939 to 1945, fought in Europe, Asia, and Africa. Great Britain, France, the United States, the Soviet Union, and their allies were on one side. Germany, Italy, Japan, and their allies were on the other side.

Websites

To learn more about Food Dudes,
visit **booklinks.abdopublishing.com**. These links are routinely monitored
and updated to provide the most current information available.

Index